What Mal Smile As Big As The Moon?

Written by Margie Kimberley
Illustrated by Michelle Marques

Read... Wonder... Smile!
Margie Kimberley

Printed in the United States of America

First Printing, 2020

Library of Congress Control Number: 2019920786
Paperback ISBN 978-1-7346479-0-7
Hardcover ISBN 978-1-7346479-1-4

Village Books Publishing
1200 Eleventh Street
Bellingham, WA 98225

To all those who read to children
and talk with them about stories.
Most especially to my mother, Olive,
who did that until she was 101. ~M.K.

In honor of my Grammy Olive – thank you
for inspiring me to pursue art for art's sake!
And to my father Steve for encouraging me to follow my dreams.
I love you and miss you both. ~M.M.

Your purchase of *What Makes You Smile as Big as the Moon?* will go to support:
1. The National Children's Book and Literacy Alliance (NCBLA)
2. Raise a Reader

The author has chosen the above national and local non-profits because of their work to support children's literacy. These agencies will receive donations from the sale of this book. Please read about each agency below and consider further supporting their good work. Thank you for believing in the importance of children's literacy efforts through your purchase of this book.

The National Children's Book and Literacy Alliance (NCBLA) is a 501(c)(3) not-for-profit organization founded by award-winning young people's authors and illustrators. Acting as an independent creative agent or with trusted partners, the NCBLA develops original projects, programs, and educational outreach that advocate for and educate about literacy, literature, libraries, the arts, and humanities. Learn more at **thencbla.org** and on Facebook (TheNCBLA).

Raise A Reader is a joint initiative of the Bellingham Public Library and Whatcom County Library System designed to prepare young children and their families for a lifetime of reading by building skills, developing interests, and fostering a love of books and stories. Raise A Reader programs include library story-times, outreach efforts such as Books for Babies, and materials for young families. Learn more at **www.bellinghampubliclibrary.org** or **www.wcls.org**

Sometimes I smile as big as the moon
when Momma makes cake in the late afternoon,

and I lick the beaters, the bowl and the spoon.

What makes you smile as big as the moon?

Sometimes I giggle
from deep down inside

When Daddy can't find me,

he's tried...

and he's tried,

Till my giggle helps show him the place where I hide.

What makes you giggle from deep down inside?

Sometimes I'm proud...
I'm strong, big and bold.
I ride my red bike,
pedal fast, feel the cold,

Then zoom a big
ZIG

ZAG,

a sight to behold!

What makes you proud... strong, big and bold?

Sometimes I wonder, go Hmmmm, and ask how
The milk in my mug got to me from the cow,

Did the cow climb into my fridge just now?

**What makes you wonder,
go Hmmmm, and ask how?**

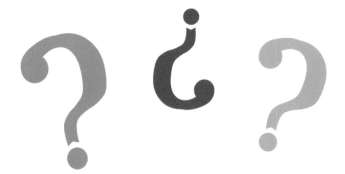

Sometimes I shout and I stomp 'cause I'm mad,

When the couch
makes a rad-rockin'
sky-jumpin' pad,

But Momma says NO,
and so does my Dad.

What makes you shout and stomp
'cause you're mad?

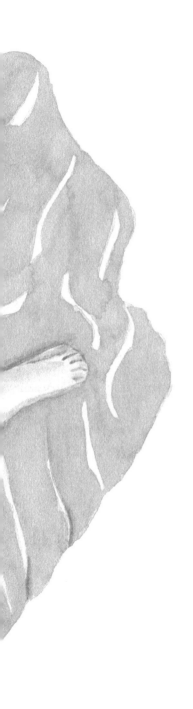

Sometimes I curl up
and just want to cry,
When I'm sad or I'm scared
or I'm hide-a-way shy,

and I need a soft hug
or a sweet lullaby.

**What makes you curl up
and just want to cry?**

Sometimes I feel I'm the best ME of all,

I'm a high flyin' hero,

I'm skyscraper **TALL!**

Nothing can stop me
or make me feel small,
nothing,
no nothing,
no nothing at all!

what makes
YOU feel you're
the best
YOU of all?

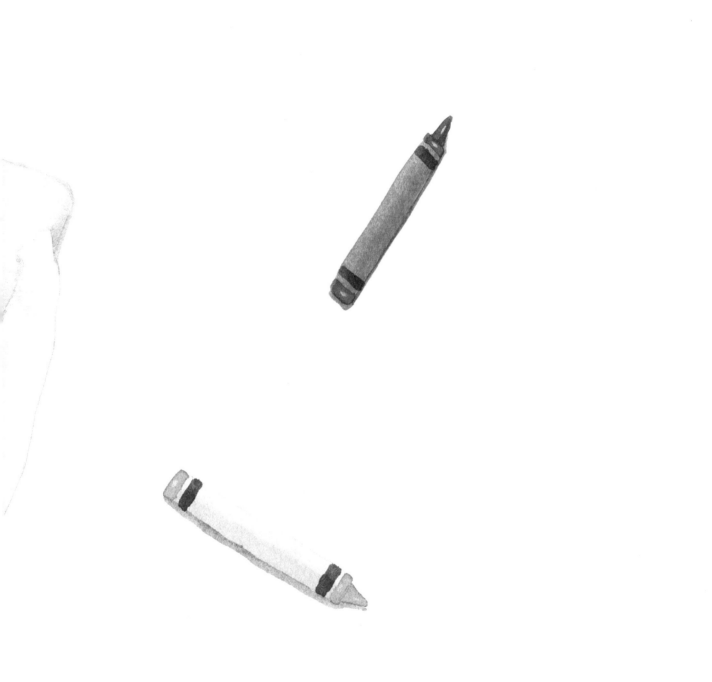

Eli is an expert tree climber and loves playing on the trampoline with his little sister, Evelyn.

Julian loves to ride his bike and pretend he is a chef!

Rachel spends her time riding horses and teaching everyone she meets about nature.

Will is curious and active! He loves to learn about history and world wars.

Hayden is an exuberant lover of life, people and family who happens to live with Down Syndrome.

Molly is a voracious reader and award-winning artist. She dreams of being a second grade teacher.

Winston is a proud dad and husband who loves his family and the Seahawks!

George goes FAST on a field, on a court, on a bike, and on a playground. He writes and plays ukulele music, and is intrigued by how things work.

Tommy is drawn to everything water - swimming, fishing, kayaks, boats and sea-life. He's also quite skilled at negotiation!

Olive dances with grace from a place deep in her soul. She keeps adults on their toes and demands the truth.

Author Bio

Margie Kimberley has lived in Wisconsin, Idaho, California, Japan and on Lummi Island. She currently resides in Bellingham, Washington with her treasure of a husband. Silly pranks or "gotchas" make her giggle from deep down inside. The state of our world right now (2020) makes her Wonder, go Hmmmm, and ask How, and her Grandchildren and their parents make her Smile as Big as the Moon.

margiekimberley.com

Illustrator Bio

Michelle Marques decided not to grow up at an early age and has been following her dreams ever since. Michelle was thrilled at the opportunity to illustrate this book with her Aunt Margie. She lives in Sonoma County, California where she hosts news and music programs on the radio. Just like the children in this book, Michelle leans into her emotions and tries hard to understand the world around her, often with her sketchbook in hand.

michellemarquesillustration.com

Guide for adults reading this book to children

Reading this book with a young child can open up a conversation about how we are growing in our awareness and understanding of our feelings and our thoughts. By wondering out loud about what happens in our everyday play activities, we can begin to think about how our feelings and thoughts influence what we do in our play.

Suggestions:

1 - Pause during the reading to discuss the questions on nearly every page. This will model to children that learning happens in supportive relationships. When you are asking and listening to children's ideas and questions, you are modeling the relationship building skills children need to form friendships and play with others.

2 - Ask if any parts of the book remind them of experiences they have had. This may lead to discussions about how we make choices based on how we are feeling and thinking.

3 - Reread the book often. This will increase the emotional vocabulary of young children and help them name and think about their feelings.

Thank you to the department of Early Childhood Education, Woodring College of Education, Western Washington University, Bellingham WA. for providing these guidelines.

CPSIA information can be obtained
at www.ICGtesting.com
Printed in the USA
LVHW070804050521
686503LV00002B/30